A PRACTICAL GUIDE TO TYING

KNOTS

How to tie 75 bends, hitches, knots, bindings, loops, mats, plaits, rings and slings in over 500 step-by-step photographs

GEOFFREY BUDWORTH

LORENZ BOOKS

This edition is published by
Lorenz Books,
an imprint of Anness Publishing Ltd,
108 Great Russell Street,
London WC1B 3NA;
info@anness.com

www.lorenzbooks.com;
www.annesspublishing.com

If you like the images in this book
and would like to investigate using
them for publishing, promotions or
advertising, please visit our website
www.practicalpictures.com for
more information.

A CIP catalogue record for this book
is available from the British Library.

Publisher Joanna Lorenz
Editorial Director Helen Sudell
Project Editor Helen Marsh
Designer Michael Morey
Production Controller Ben Worley

Previously published as part of a larger
volume, *Simple Knots & Basic Ropework*

PUBLISHER'S NOTE

Although the advice and information
in this book are believed to be accurate
and true at the time of going to press,
neither the authors nor the publisher
can accept any legal responsibility or
liability for any errors or omissions
that may have been made nor for any
inaccuracies nor for any loss, harm or
injury that comes about from following
instructions or advice in this book.

Contents

CAUTION

Do not use any of the knots, bends, hitches, etc., in this book for a purpose that
involves forseeable risk of loss, damage or injury without the appropriate training and
equipment. Cavers, climbers, rescue workers, wilderness or ocean-going adventurers
who wish to use a particular knot for those (or any other) activities and pursuits are
strongly advised to seek the advice of qualified practitioners first. This book is
intended only to be a simple introduction to knot-tying.

INTRODUCTION

Knotting is an enjoyable pastime. Most people can learn to tie knots, and even the complete beginner can soon acquire an impressive repertoire of useful or merely decorative knots. Knot tying is as absorbing as reading a good book, and the end product is as satisfactory as a completed crossword or jigsaw puzzle – but with many more practical applications. Everyone ought to know a few knots; that is why the International Guild of Knot Tyers (IGKT), founded in 1982, is now a recognized educational charity. Nobody should be over-dependent upon safety pins and superglues, patent zips (zippers) and clips and other fastenings, when a suitable length of cord and the right combination of knots are cheaper, consume less of the planet's scarce energy resources, and often work better. Knot tying can also be great fun! There are several thousand individual knots and an almost infinite number of variations of some of them. In addition, new knots emerge every year from the fingers of innovative knot tyers to increase the existing numbers. Then there are the ornamental aspects: macramé; leather-braiding and whipmaking; Chinese decorative knotting; Japanese *kumihimo* and other elaborate braiding or plaiting techniques; traditional British corn dollies; tassels, tatting and crocheting. Magicians and escapologists practise knot and rope trickery. Mathematicians venture into three dimensions when they explore the abstruse topological field of knot theory. Knotting is a delightful pursuit, and with a little guidance the novice can soon become adept at many new techniques. This book does not aim to cover everything outlined above, but the 100 or so carefully chosen knots it contains will act as an invaluable introduction to the subject. Those who wish to learn a few basic knots for practical use will find this an essential handbook, and others who want to learn to tie more elaborate knots will be able to progress from this comprehensive introduction on to more challenging knot-tying techniques.

KEY TO KNOT USER GROUPS

Angling/Fishing	
Boating/Sailing	
Caving/Climbing	
General Purpose	
Outdoor Pursuits	

Materials

A lefthanded (or S-laid) cable consists of three righthanded (Z-laid) hawsers. Each of these ropes has three lefthanded (counterclockwise) strands made from numerous righthanded (clockwise) yarns, spun from vegetable fibres.

Rope has been made by man since the Stone Age, utilising the materials that were available. European hunter-gatherers, 10,000 years ago, grew only one crop – flax – and that was for rope, not food; the ancient Egyptians and Persians made rope from papyrus and flax. Even a captive orang-utan is reported to have made a kind of rope from its bedding material and then swung from it.

It is no surprise that man has gone to such lengths to develop and enhance rope-making materials. Rope enabled humankind to probe the deepest caves and to seek fuel and ores in underground mines; to migrate over rugged terrain with pack animals; to capture, harness and ride other beasts; to sail and cross oceans in search of treasure, trade, conquest and colonization. Rope concentrated the efforts of the labour force that built the great Egyptian pyramids and created the blocks and tackles with which medieval European stone masons erected their Gothic cathedrals and castles.

VEGETABLE FIBRE CORDAGE

As we have seen, until this century, rope was made from the shredded, combed and graded fibres of plant stems such as flax and jute, or from the leaves of sisal and abaca (hemp). It was made from fibres attached to seeds (cotton), and from other vegetable materials as diverse as fibrous coconut shells (coir),

horse and camel (even human) hair, date palms, reeds, esparto grass, wool and silk.

Because of its origins in nature, such cordage is also referred to as natural fibre. These fibres were spun clockwise (or righthanded) to create long yarns. Several of these yarns were next twisted up anticlockwise (counterclockwise) into strands. Finally, three strands were laid up clockwise or righthanded which created a typical rope.

The incurably romantic – who wish that square-rigged sailing ships were still commonplace – regret the demise of these vegetable fibre ropes, with their evocative smells and every shade of gold and brown; but, with the emergence of synthetic (manmade) cordage, the shortcomings of natural fibre ropes became intolerable. They were comparatively weak, even when scaled up to enormous diameters. Unable to withstand

SYNTHETIC (MANMADE) ROPE

A 14 mm (⁷⁄₁₂ in) diameter, soft matt polyester, 16-plait sheath encloses a hawser-laid core of several thousand high-tenacity polyester filaments.

Vegetable fibre knotted cordage in its natural element.

Natural fibre ropes vary in colour and may be blonde or brunette.

much abrasion, vegetable fibre cordage was also prey to mildew, rot, insects and vermin. It swelled when wet (so knots became impossible to untie) and froze in icy conditions with irreparable weakening as brittle fibres broke. Such ropes were also rough on the hands.

Obtainable only from specialized sources, and at a premium price, the use of natural fibre cordage is now very limited, – except in situations (such as filming a costume drama, rigging a classic wooden boat, and designing the interior decor and window dressing of nautical pubs, clubs and restaurants) where the appearance of an earlier period must be evoked. Some thoughtful

souls, however, concerned by what they perceive to be a profligate use of the earth's finite resources, prophesy an eventual return to natural fibre cordage, the raw materials of which can be harvested from renewable growing crops, without destructive ecological footprints.

Sisal rope is still sold for general purposes. Children shin up best-quality soft hemp ropes in school gyms. Coir is used for boat fenders. And for weather-resistant serving and seizing of wire and rope rigging by professional riggers, balls of tarred hemp spun yarn are still sold in several sizes.

It used to be that a rope could only be as long as the ropewalk (open field or long shed) where it

was made – although, of course, two or more could then be spliced together – but compact modern machinery has overcome this and, with extruded synthetic filaments, rope of practically any length can be made.

SYNTHETIC (MANMADE) CORDAGE

Discovered and developed by research chemists in the 1930s, the basic elements for synthetic cordage are: very fine continuous clusters of multifilaments, less than 50 microns/$\frac{1}{500}$ in across and of uniform diameter and circular cross-section; coarser monofilaments, individually more than 50 microns/$\frac{1}{500}$ in in diameter; discontinuous staple fibres (from

◆ LEFT
Sisal fibres are rough and hairy, but soft to the touch.

◆ BELOW
Cordage lengths are no longer limited by the extent of the ropewalk, either field or long shed, where it was made.

Terylene and Dacron); polypropylene, which is best for mundane domestic use; polyethylene (or Polythene), often sold as balls of twine; and a few so-called "miracle fibres" (such as Kevlar, Dyneema or Spectra) representing the latest and more expensive cutting edge of ropemaking technology. There are two grades of nylon: Nylon 66, discovered in the Du Pont laboratories, was the first manmade fibre of merit available to the cordage industry, and Nylon 6, subsequently developed by I.G. Farbenindustrie. Terylene was a British development from investigations at the Calico Printers Association, the sole rights were then taken up by Imperial Chemical Industries.

2 cm/⅝ in to 2 m/2 yd in length) made by cutting multifilaments or monofilaments into discrete lengths; and flat, narrow, ribbon-like strings produced from extruded split or fibrillated film. The brightly coloured balls of twine often found in hardware shops and stores are usually split film products, as are the larger balls and cops (cylindrical reels) sold at garden centres for horticulture use or as baling twines for agricultural machinery.

All of these raw materials make cordage that is size-for-size stronger and lighter than its vegetable fibre equivalent. A three-strand nylon rope is more than twice as strong as a manila one, yet it weighs half as much and may last four to five times as long. Many can be dyed a variety of colours (even including psychedelic patterns). Almost as strong when wet, they have a high tensile (breaking) strength and are also able to withstand sudden shock loading. Although not

plagued by the ills that afflict natural fibre ropes, they are more susceptible to heat generated by friction – softening, melting and even parting in extreme cases.

The most common manmade materials are: polyamide (nylon), the strongest man-made cordage; polyester (best known trade names

◆ RIGHT
Man-made cordage is smoother than
natural yarn, but stronger.

MANMADE MATERIALS

"MIRACLE FIBRES"

Kevlar – discovered by Du Pont as long ago as 1965 – is an organic polymer immune to moisture and rot. Weight-for-weight it is twice as strong as nylon, but with low elasticity, and it has been used to replace wire halyards. Then there is Spectra or HMPE, the brand name of Allied Chemicals who manufactured this super-lightweight polyethylene (marketed by others as Dyneema and Admiral 2000). Its phenomenal tensile strength is greater than that of stainless steel. Released in 1985, it looks set to supersede Kevlar. The considerable cost of these will not deter ocean yacht racers or climbers, for whom competitive edge and extra safety margins are worth any price, but they are not recommended for routine knot tying.

POLYAMIDE (NYLON)

Polyamide is the strongest manmade cordage (although 10–15 per cent less when wet) and cheaper than polyester. It is very elastic, stretching under a load anything from 10 per cent to 40 per cent, then regaining its original length when the load is removed. This makes it suitable for mooring lines, also towing and rock-climbing ropes – but not in the restricted space of caves or crowded moorings, where stretchy ropes could be a liability. It does not float, so nylon can also be used for yachting anchor warps. The best colour to buy is white, as colouring may weaken the fibres by 10 per cent (while

certainly adding a lot to the price). A fairly high melting point of up to 260°C (478°F) ensures a reduced risk of melting due to friction; but be warned, it will, like all synthetics, soften and be irredeemably weakened at a much lower temperature than its melting point. Polyamide withstands attack from alkalis (and acids, to a lesser degree), oils and organic solvents. It has acceptable resistance to photochemical degradation from the ultra-violet wavelengths in sunlight, and to abrasion. Domestic consumers of this product will be impressed to learn that it is recommended for deep-sea towing and widely used in the off-shore oil industry.

POLYESTER (TERYLENE, DACRON)

Three-quarters the strength of nylon (but equally strong wet or dry), polyester does not stretch half as much, and pre-stretching during manufacture can remove most of the latent elasticity it does possess. Consequently it is recommended for standing rigging, sheets and halyards, where stretch is unwanted but high tensile strength is required, even replacing wire. It resists acids (and alkalis, to a lesser extent), oils and organic solvents. Like nylon, it does not float and it has about the same melting point and resistance to sunlight – but polyester wears better.

POLYETHYLENE (POLYTHENE)

Cheap, light (but it barely floats in water), without much stretch,

polyethylene is fairly hard-wearing and durable but has the lowest melting point of the four "poly" materials. It is sold in hardware stores as balls of twine and is used in the fishing industry, but it is too stiff and springy for most knot tying.

POLYPROPYLENE

In terms of cost and performance, this cordage may be ranked between vegetable fibre and the superior (nylon, terylene) manmade fibre cordage. Made from multifilament, monofilament, staple fibre or split film, it is the most versatile of synthetic fibres. Large quantities are manufactured and sold, at reasonable prices, via hardware and DIY shops and stores for all kinds of mundane work entailing no high performance risks. It has one-third to half the breaking strength of nylon and a much lower melting point – around 150°C (302°F) – rendering it useless for any task where friction generates anything approaching that amount of heat, but, as it is the lightest of the synthetics, and floats indefinitely, it is the obvious choice for lifelines and water-skiing towlines. It is completely rot-proof and resistant to most acids, alkalis and oils, but affected adversely by bleaching agents and some industrial solvents, while some cheaper brands denature in bright sun. For lovers of traditional cordage, there is a light brown rope – reliable, hardwearing and inexpensive – made from polypropylene to resemble hemp.

Breaking Strengths

Ropemakers' brochures and leaflets usually contain tables listing the minimum average breaking load of every type and size of their cordage products. Unfortunately, the data differs from company to company, depending upon the tests and equipment each firm uses, making comparisons difficult.

SPECIFICATIONS

Product specifications may blur the facts: for example, a "mooring line", made for specialized markets, may consist of an elastic nylon core inside a hard-wearing polyester sheath, while many mass-produced and comparatively cheap cordage items, sold for the domestic market, can be much weaker. Nevertheless, an appreciation of the main rope and cordage

species can be gained from the following outline. The minimum breaking strength of a 4 mm/⅙ in diameter slim nylon cord of 3-strand or 8-plait construction is likely to be around 320 kg/705 lb, which might withstand two 159-kg/25-stone Japanese sumo wrestlers having a tug-of-war. For standard 3-strand polyester of the same diameter the figure is a trifle lower – 295 kg/650 lb – but an 8-plait construction combined with pre-stretch treatment changes that to around 450 kg/990 lb. Polypropylene of the same diameter is variously quoted at 140 kg/309 lb, 250 kg/551 lb and even 430 kg/925 lb; polyethylene is about 185 kg/408 lb, while the average breaking strength of a 4 mm/⅙ in cord of Dyneema/Admiral 2000/Spectra is a remarkable 650 kg/1,432 lb. To

achieve these kinds of performance with natural fibres, it would be necessary to have at least a 25 per cent increase in diameter to 5 mm/⅕ in manila or 33.3 per cent to 6 mm/¼ in sisal.

LARGER SIZES

With a 10 mm/⁵⁄₁₂ in thin nylon 3-strand hawser, the minimum breaking strength increases to around 2,400 kg/5,292 lb. That is almost two-and-a-half metric tonnes, the weight of a large motor vehicle. Again, the average figure is somewhat less for polyester at 2,120 kg/about 2 tons; 1,382 kg/1⅓ tons for polypropylene; and 1,090 kg/ just over a ton for polyethelene. Dyneema/Admiral 2000/Spectra, by contrast, would be about 4,000 kg/about 4 tons. The same size of rope in manila could only cope with 710 kg/1,565 lb and sisal with 635 kg/1,400 lb.

Finally, for a sizeable 24 mm/ 1 in rope diameter, the average quoted breaking strengths are: nylon = 13 tonnes/12.8 tons; polyester = 10 tonnes/9.8 tons; polypropylene = 8 tonnes/7.9 tons; polyethylene = 6 tonnes/5.9 tons; and Dyneema/Admiral 2000/Spectra = a stupendous 20 tonnes/19.7 tons. Even the best manila would have to be nearly twice that size (and four times as strong) to match those figures.

◆ LEFT
Vegetable fibre cordage is much weaker and generally has a shorter life than synthetic products.

COMPARING AND CONTRASTING NATURAL FIBRE AND SYNTHETIC FIBRE ROPES

	NATURAL FIBRES				SYNTHETIC FIBRES			
	Sisal	Cotton	Hemp	Manilla	Polyethylene	Polypropylene	Polyester	Polyamide
Shock loading	●	●	●●●	●●	●	●●●	●●	●●●●
Handling	●	●●●●	●●●	●●	●●●	●●●	●●●●	●●●●
Durability	●	●●	●●●●	●●●	●●	●●●	●●●●	●●●●
Rot & mildew resistance	●	●	●	●	●●●●	●●●●	●●●●	●●●●
U.V. resistance	●●●●	●●●●	●●●●	●●●●	●●	●	●●●●	●●
Acid resistance	●	●	●	●	●●●●	●●●●	●●●●	●●●
Alkali resistance	●●	●●	●●	●●	●●●●	●●●●	●●●●	●●●●
Abrasion resistance	●●	●●	●●●	●●●	●●	●●	●●●●	●●●●
Storage	dry	dry	dry	dry	wet or dry	wet or dry	wet or dry	wet or dry
Buoyancy	sinks	sinks	sinks	sinks	floats (just)	floats	sinks	sinks
Melting point*	not affected	not affected	not affected	not affected	about 128°C (about 262°F)	about 150°C (about 302°F)	about 245°C (about 473°F)	about 250°C (about 482°F)

Key: ● poor ●● acceptable ●●● good ●●●● excellent
* Note that cordage softens and weakens at perhaps 20–30 per cent lower temperatures.

SUMMARY

These data take no account of fair wear and tear (including knots), damage or misuse (e.g. shock loading, or excessive friction). Consequently a safe working load will be considerably less – perhaps a fifth to a seventh of the quoted strengths. Then again, it is often necessary to buy synthetic cordage many times stronger than actually required; for example, a 4 mm/⅙ in cord would not match a block and tackle made for 25 mm/1 in rope even though it might be able to cope with the intended load, nor could it be comfortably grasped in the hand and heaved.

Knot tyers do not normally need to know either the molecular structure of cordage or its test data interpreted in charts and graphs. Cavers and climbers, flyers (of gliders and microlight aircraft), and all who calculatingly engage in potentially hazardous pursuits – from astronautics to undersea exploration – can obtain these technical details from the manufacturers. For the average user, a general knowledge of the main types of cordage is all that is needed to buy shrewdly and sensibly.

Tools

Tying elaborate knots is made easier
with one or more handy tools (see key
to illustration).

Acquire a sharp and robust craft
knife to cut rope and cord;
scissors work only on thin strings
and twines. Most of the knots in
this book can be tied and
tightened with just the fingers,
aided now and then with a prod
from the pointed cap of a
ballpoint pen. A few of the
slightly trickier knots are more
easily completed with one or
more of the following tools.

GRIPFIDS
Handmade by rope craftsman
Stuart Grainger, these resemble
small Swedish fids, with the
refinement that the tip clings to
working strands, pulling them
through knotwork as the tool is
withdrawn. Two sizes cope with
cordage up to either 7 mm/³⁄₁₀ in
or 12 mm/¹⁄₂ in diameter.

NETTING NEEDLES
These serve as bobbins for storing
quantities of small cords tangle-
free and ready for immediate use.
Sizes range from a tiny 11.5 cm/
4¹⁄₂ in to jumbo-sized ones 30 cm/
12 in or more in length. Shun
crudely made ones in favour of
those that are polished to a
smooth finish. The seller will
show you how to load them.

ROUND-BILLED PLIERS
Handy for tightening knots with
lots of crossing points. Most high
street hardware shops or do-it-
yourself superstores will have
them. Choose a pair to suit the
scale of work: a small size
(sometimes called "jeweller's

pliers") will have an overall
length of about 10 cm/4 in,
with more robust sizes from
about 15 cm/6 in upwards.

SWEDISH FIDS*
These are used to poke and prize
open gaps through which
working strands can be tucked
and pulled. Obtainable from
yacht chandlers and serious rope
stockists, they range in length
from about 15 cm/6 in to 38 cm/
15 in or more. Choose a size to
match the scale of your work.

WIRE LOOPS
Homemade from stiff and springy
wire 0.25 cm/¹⁄₁₀ in diameter – or
thinner – inserted securely into a
handle, these are indispensable
alternatives to fids when working
with smaller stuff.

KEY TO TOOLS	
1	Netting needle (large)
2	Netting needle (medium)
3	Netting needle (small)
4	Gripfid (large)
5	Gripfid (small)
6	Hollow "Swedish" fid (small)
7	Hollow "Swedish" fid (large)
8	Homemade wire loop (large)
9	Homemade wire loop (small)
10	Homemade wire loop (medium)
11	Jeweller's pliers
12	Round-billed pliers

* Originally fids were solid
hardwood spikes. They can
occasionally be found in antique
shops or markets as collectable
treen (lathe-turned wood).

Cutting & Securing Ends

TYING & TAPING

Before cutting any natural fibre cordage, first tape or tie it to prevent fraying. Adhesive tape is the least attractive option – and unacceptable on finished craftwork – but it is used a lot in preparatory stages as an easy alternative to whipping. Wrap where the cut is to be made and then simply slice the tape in half to achieve two bound ends at a stroke. Alternatively, tie a pair of strangle or constrictor knots, one on either side of where the cut is to be made.

HEATING & SEALING

This is now widely practised by ropeworkers and riggers. There is no need to tape or tie heat-sealed ends. Rope manufacturers and stockists have electrically heated guillotines to cut-and-seal the ropes and cords they sell. These cost too much for most of us, so the comparatively cool yellow flame of a struck match may have to do on small stuff. For large diameters, or to cut-and-seal a batch of strands, heat the blade of an old penknife in the blue flame of a blow-torch until the tip and edge glow cherry-red. Pause to re-heat it every few seconds for a clean and fast cut. Nylon melts, drips and burns with whitish smoke and a smell said to resemble fish or celery; it may even flash into a small flame (easily blown out). Polyester melts, drips and burns with dense black smoke and a smell like mushrooms. Polypropylene and

TYING

1 Tie two constrictor knots, one either side of where the cut will be made.

TAPING

1 Wrap a turn or two of adhesive tape around the rope or cord.

2 Slice vertically down halfway between the two binding knots already tied.

2 Cut vertically down through the middle of the taped portion.

HEAT SEALING 1

With an electric guillotine or a heated knife blade (not shown), cordage and small diameter ropes may be neatly cut and sealed.

HEAT SEALING 2

Use the naked flame of a match or cigarette lighter for a quick but often lumpy seal.

polyethylene react at lower temperatures, shrinking rapidly away from the source of heat. It is possible to pinch the soft heated ends to a point, rolling them between forefinger and thumb, before they harden, but take care

to wet the fingertips first or it may cause a burn and blister. A cord that appears to be synthetic but actually chars and even ignites without melting, is probably made from rayon, which comes from wood pulp.

Terms & Techniques

Anyone who ties a knot is described in knotting circles as a tyer (not tier) since the former is unambiguous while the latter has a different meaning when written.

SIMPLE TERMS

The end actively involved in the tying process is referred to as the **working end** or sometimes – by anglers – as the **tag end**; the in-active remainder is known as the **standing part** and **standing end**. Doubling a line so that two parts are brought close together creates a **bight**. If this is done to locate the exact centre of the bit of stuff in hand, then one is said to **middle** it. Once the two adjacent parts cross, a bight turns into a loop; a further twist creates a couple of **elbows**, while the process of turning a bight or loop into an improvised eye by wrapping the end several times around the standing part is referred to as **dogging**. Any loop that is pulled

NOTE

Several categories of knots in this book have been illustrated in thicker cordage than would ordinarily be used to tie them. For instance, the whippings and fishermen's knots would actually be tied in very fine twines and monofilaments. This has been done to make the tying process clearer. The characteristically barrel-shaped knots for use in angling monofilaments do not always tighten as easily in larger cordage – but they can, with a little more time and care, be shaped and tightened to make useful general purpose holdfasts.

so small that it deforms and damages a rope becomes a **kink**.

The word **rope** is generally defined as meaning any plaited, braided or laid (in strands) product over 10 mm ($5/12$ in) in diameter, although there are exceptions (for example, some climbing ropes are 9 mm/$3/8$ in diameter). Anything much smaller is referred to as **cord**, **string**, **twine** or **thread**. Rope and cord are collectively called **cordage** but, more commonly, **stuff**. A rope or cord dedicated to a particular job becomes a **line** (tow line, washing line, lifeline, throwing or heaving line), or acquires an even more specific label (lanyard, lashing or lassoo). A lightweight throwing or heaving line that is used to haul a heavier line across an intervening space is known as a **messenger**. The terms **plait** and **braid** are virtually interchangeable. There are, however, some who say that braids are flat while plaits have a three-dimensional cross-section.

Ropeworkers often "take a **turn**" in order to check a load by means of the friction it applies. Wrapping the working end an extra amount to bring it alongside the standing part, so as to tie it off, produces a **round turn**. Converting a single-ply knot to two, three (or more) ply involves following the original **lead** of the knot around with the working end. The place within a knot where the collective friction of its parts is concentrated is known as the **nip**. The tuck that finally secures a knot, preventing it from collapsing or unravelling, is the **locking tuck**. A simple loop is an **overhand loop** when the working end lies on top of the standing part, becoming an **underhand loop** if the working end goes beneath the standing part.

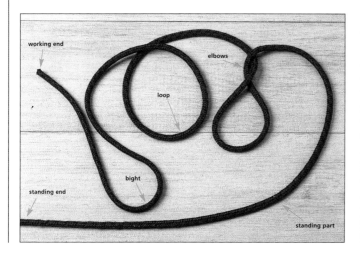

working end

elbows

loop

bight

standing end

standing part

1 More often than not, a clove hitch may have been tied with the working end.

2 But slide the knot sideways off its foundation – and it will fall apart.

3 Once separated from its foundation, nothing remains of the knot but the line in which it was tied.

4 To re-tie the clove hitch, this time in the bight, first cast an overhand loop.

5 Create a second underhand loop immediately alongside the first one.

6 Twist the loops to overlap them. The resulting clove hitch may be slid back on to its foundation.

TYING TECHNIQUES

Most knots can be tied in more than one way. The methods illustrated have been chosen either because they are easier to learn or to photograph clearly. Practised knot tyers develop more dextrous ways to tie knots that are almost sleight of hand. Discover these slicker and quicker tying tricks for yourself: with a completed knot in your hands, back-track, untying the knot a step at a time, to see how it is

created. A short cut may occur to you. Re-tie it that way in future.

Tying a knot "in the bight" means doing so without using the working end. When a hitch or a binding knot collapses to nothing if slid from the foundation around which it was tied or a loop knot can be unravelled without recourse to its ends (in other words, it "unties in the bight"), then it can be tied in the bight. This is the "law of hitch & bight" proposed by Harry Asher in the

mid-1980s. A surprising number of knots may be tied this way. Knowing the principle can also enable knot tyers to spot subtle differences in seemingly identical knots: for example, the bag knot can be tied in the bight but the miller's knot cannot.

Most knots must be drawn up gradually so as to remove slack and daylight before gently pulling on each end and standing part in turn to create a knot that remains snug and firm.

Basic Knots, Bends & Hitches

SIMPLE, OVERHAND OR THUMB KNOT

This is the most elementary stopper knot, to prevent small stuff (cotton, thread or string) from fraying or pulling out of a hole through which it has been threaded. Its uses range from securing thread in a needle to tying loose change into the corner of a handkerchief when on the beach or anywhere else where deep pockets are temporarily not available. Nobody ever has to be taught to tie this knot. It just comes naturally.

1 Make an overhand loop in the small stuff that is to be tied.

2 Tuck the working end through the loop already formed and pull on the standing end to tighten the knot.

OVERHAND KNOT WITH DRAWLOOP

Drawloops act as quick releases, and may also strengthen some knots by bulking them up with an extra knot part. Overlooked and underrated by many knot tyers, drawloops deserve to be used more, and will from time to time be recommended in this book.

Start to tie a simple overhand knot but stop before the working end has been fully pulled through.

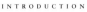

TWO STRAND OVERHAND KNOT

This is another knot that the youngest person can tie instinctively. It creates a bigger stopper knot, for cottons or domestic string, and also acts to hold cords together as long as they lie in the same direction, for example, to prevent a waist tie in pyjamas, swimming trunks or tracksuit trousers (sweatpants) from pulling out when not in use. NB: This is not a bend because the two cords are not aligned to be pulled in opposite directions.

1 Place the two strings or cords to be tied parallel and together.

2 Tie a simple overhand knot. Tighten, taking care to keep the lines parallel (like railway tracks) throughout.

DOUBLE OVERHAND KNOT

This forms a chunkier stopper knot than the simple overhand knot, although it will not block a larger hole. It is, however, an indispensable technique for other knots that are based upon it.

1 Tie an overhand knot – but tuck the working end a second time.

2 Gently pull both ends apart, at the same time twisting them in opposite directions. In the example shown, the lefthand thumb goes up and away from the tyer, the righthand thumb down and away. The cord dictates what it wants to do; simply go along with it. See how a diagonal knot part wraps itself around – let it happen. Pull on both ends at the same time to tighten this knot.

OVERHAND BEND

Also known as the tape knot, this knot is recommended for the flat or tubular woven webbing (tape) used by cavers and climbers – although it works in anything from the largest cables to the finest angling monofilaments.

2 Follow the lead of the original knot with the second working end.

3 For a twofold knot, it may be stronger if the short ends are at the top. Pull the standing parts to tighten.

1 Tie an overhand knot in the end of one of the two lines to be joined. Insert the end of the second line.

FISHERMAN'S KNOT

The reliable fisherman's knot can be used for anything and everything from domestic to heavy industrial tasks. This is a knot that can be untied if it has been made from rope, but if you make it out of string you will have to cut it off.

1 Lay the two lines parallel and close to one another, tying an overhand knot with one end around the standing part of the other.

2 Turn the half-completed knot end-for-end and tie an identical overhand knot with the other end. Pull first on both working ends to tighten the individual knots, then on the standing parts to unite and tighten the knot.

SINGLE HITCH

Commonly referred to as a half hitch, alone this is an unreliable means of attachment except for the most temporary and trivial of purposes (when a drawloop might help) but it is the means of finishing off other more substantial working hitches.

1 Tie the ubiquitous overhand knot around something firm, such as a fat felt tip pen, to discover how this careful rearrangement traps the working end.

2 Leave a longer working end, which is not completely pulled through, for a drawloop.

TWO HALF HITCHES

Two half hitches are the tried and trusted way to secure a line to a ring, rail or anything. They are always identical, i.e. the working end goes the same way around the standing part in both cases.

1 Tie a single half hitch with the working end of the line.

2 Add an identical second half hitch and draw them snugly together to complete this useful attachment.

ROUND TURN & TWO HALF HITCHES

This is a classic hitch, comparatively strong and secure, the name of which describes it exactly. It can be used to secure a boat, to tow a broken-down vehicle or secure a load.

1 Take a turn around the anchorage, bring the working end alongside the standing part, and apply a half hitch.

2 Add an identical half hitch to complete this dependable knot.

OVERHAND KNOT & HALF HITCH

This loop knot has been used by weavers to rig looms, by Inuits (Eskimos) to string bows, by anglers as a leader loop for tackle, and for starting to tie parcels. It is sometimes called a packer's knot.

1 Tie an overhand knot with a large drawloop. Adjust the loop to the required size.

2 Wrap and tuck a half hitch with the working end around the standing part. Tighten by pulling on each one of the loop legs in turn.

OVERHAND LOOP

Use this very basic knot in thin stuff for starting parcels and other lashings. It does not easily untie and is therefore a knot that must generally be cut off and discarded after use.

1 Double one end of a cord (make a bight) and form a loop in the doubled end.

2 Tie an overhand knot, taking the trouble to keep the knot parts neatly parallel throughout the knot. Tighten by pulling on each one of the four knot parts in turn.

SIMPLE NOOSE

This simplest of running (sliding) loops is useful to start parcels or other lashings.

Working away from the short end, tie an overhand knot (with drawloop) in what would normally be regarded as the standing part of the line, and pull it tight.

BENDS & HITCHES

A bend is any knot that joins two ropes or other lines together. A line is said to be "made fast" (not "hitched") to various objects, even another rope, and only the knot itself is called a hitch. As a general rule, it should be possible to untie bends after use, for rope is a costly item that may be re-used. Restrict knots that can't be untied to string, anglers' monofilaments and other such material, from which they can be cut off and discarded. Most bends are made in two separate ends of identical material but some are intended for use when two lines differ noticeably in diameter or stiffness. The lightweight binding knots that join the two ends of the same length of line (for example, shoe laces) are knots – as opposed to bends – but in more substantial knots, bends are employed to create cargo strops and, of course, endless slings for caving and climbing.

Flemish Bend

Old seamen viewed this bend with disfavour, because it tended to jam in natural fibre ropes, but it suits synthetic cordage. Climbers like it because it is easily learned and readily checked by a team leader.

1 Make a loop in one end of one of the two lines to be joined.

2 Impart half a twist, in this instance left thumb going up and away – that is, anticlockwise (counterclockwise).

3 Tuck the working end as shown to create the characteristic figure-of-eight outline.

4 Introduce the second line, with its working end parallel to and alongside the first one.

5 Follow the lead of the first rope with the second, keeping to the outside of the first bend (evidence suggests that this makes a stronger knot).

6 Continue around and through the original knot, transferring to the inside of the second bend.

7 Complete the two-ply knot, then tighten it a bit at a time by pulling on each working end and standing part in turn.

Double Figure-of-Eight Bend

This knot is similar in function to the fisherman's knot but, unlike that knot, it is bilaterally symmetrical (both sides look the same). Several knots with a figure-of-eight layout are referred to as Flemish knots, and an alternative name for this one is the Flemish bend. Leave the knots a few inches apart for a knot that will absorb a sudden jerk or snatch by sliding before it holds.

1 Tie a figure-of-eight knot in one of the two lines and insert the second line through the first knot.

2 Then begin to tie another figure-of-eight knot.

3 Complete the second figure-of-eight knot, which, when the work is turned end-for-end, must be identical to the first one.

4 Pull first on the working ends to remove the slack from the individual knots, then on both standing parts to slide them together.

Double Harness Bend with Parallel Ends

Many knot tyers prefer
symmetrical bends, which are
often better looking and can be
easier to learn, tie and memorize.
This version is also a little
stronger and more secure than
some asymetrical knots.

1 Place the two lines to be joined
parallel and together.

2 Take one working end down
beneath the other standing part.

3 Then bring this end up and back
over the other line.

4 Tuck the end down between
both lines to complete one half
of the knot.

5 Turn the half-completed knot end-
for-end and tie an identical crossing
knot with the other working end. Work
the knot tight, so that both ends protrude
together from the same side of the knot.

Strop Bend

Any two eyes, loops and endless strops or slings may be interlaced this way. It can amuse young children to make long multi-coloured chains of elastic bands with a series of these knots; but the strop bend can also be put to hard labour on construction sites and dockyards.

1 Bring together two bights and insert one up through the other.

2 Double the working bight of the two back upon itself.

3 Pick up the standing parts of the working loop to draw them through the secondary loop.

4 Pull the remainder of the working loop completely through itself.

5 Begin to pull the two bights in opposite directions, one away from the other.

6 Continue until the two bights are snugly interlocked with one another.

7 Tighten by pulling on both pairs of loop legs at once. While this knot resembles a reef (square) knot in layout, the dynamics are very different, and it will, of course, only come undone if one of the lines breaks.

Carrick Bend with Ends Opposed

This knot name dates from the 18th century, but its actual origin is obscure. At Carrick-on-Suir in Ireland, the Elizabethan plasterwork of Ormonde Castle is embellished with numerous carrick bends moulded in relief, while a "carrack" was a type of medieval trading ship, from which perhaps comes Carrick Road outside Falmouth Harbour in Cornwall. Recommended for large hawsers and cables, this bend has acquired a reputation for strength, when it actually reduces the breaking strength of the ropes to about 65 per cent. Nevertheless, given today's strong synthetic cordages, it is still a considerable heavyweight among bends. It is said to be more secure if it is tied in such a way that the working ends emerge on opposite sides of the knot.

1 Make a loop with the working end of one of the two lines to be joined lying (in this instance) over its own standing part.

2 Place the second line over the initial loop, in the direction shown, and pass the working end beneath the other standing part.

3 Begin a second loop, taking the second working end over the first working end.

4 With the second end, make a locking tuck that goes under-over-under to complete the knot. Pull on the two standing parts to tighten the knot, when the flat heraldic outline will capsize into a compact and different form.

Carrick Bend with Ends Adjacent

With the ends on the same side of the knot, the carrick bend becomes the heraldic device once known as the Wake knot, the badge of the Saxon leader Hereward the Wake who in 1071 AD revolted against William the Conqueror. The late Desmond Mandeville, who researched the relationships of bends for more than 25 years, discovered there was one knot to which all were related and to which every family tree he drew returned – this one. Use this knot for decorative purposes, retaining the flat and open layout. It can look most attractive when used as a curtain tie-back, to secure a dressing gown cord, or even on an antique chaise longue.

1 Make a loop with the working end of one of the two lines to be joined going over the standing part.

2 Lay the working end of the second line beneath the initial loop, pointing in the direction shown.

3 Bring the second working end over the other working end.

4 Begin a second loop by taking the second new working end under the other standing part.

5 Make a locking tuck that goes over-under-over to secure the lefthand half of the knot.

6 Unlike the ends opposed version, keep this knot flat and open.

Sheet Bend

This knot is neither strong nor secure. It reduces the strength of lines by 55 per cent, and can spill if subject to spasmodic jerking. This said, it is part of every knot tyer's basic repertoire. When it attaches a lanyard to a loop it may be referred to as a becket hitch, and, tied (by a different method) in yarns, it is called the weaver's knot.

1 Create a bight in the end of one of the ropes to be tied.

2 Take the second rope and tuck it up through the bight.

3 Pass the working end beneath the bight.

4 Tuck the working end beneath itself in such a way that both short ends are located on the same side of the completed knot (with many materials, it seems to be more secure this way).

Double Sheet Bend

If the two lines are of dissimilar size or stiffness, make the bight in the bigger or tougher one, and tie this double sheet bend to counteract any tendency for it to straighten and so spill the knot. There is no need for a third tuck. If this knot is insufficient, try the racking bend.

1 Make a bight in the larger of the two ropes to be joined.

2 Take the second of the lines and tuck it up through the bight.

3 Bring the end around and beneath the bight in the other rope.

4 Tuck the working end beneath itself so that both short ends are located on the same side of the knot (with many materials it is more secure this way).

5 Bring the working end around and beneath the bight and its own standing line once again, keeping it to the right of the original pass.

6 Finally, tuck the end through alongside the initial tuck to complete the double knot.

One-Way Sheet Bend

When a sheet bend is likely to be dragged over or through obstructions, the two short ends can be streamlined by means of this adaption. Use this simple but effective modification for ropes that may be towed in water, passed through a rocky crevice or even exposed to gale-force winds. The three short ends should, of course, point away from the direction in which the knot is being pulled so that they will not be pulled by the current or catch against any rocks.

1 Make a bight with the working end of one of the two ropes to be joined.

3 Pass the working end around and beneath the bight in the other rope.

2 Take the end of the other rope and tuck it up through the bight.

4 Tuck the end beneath itself so both short ends are on the same side.

5 Then bring the working end around and back on itself again to make a figure-of-eight.

6 Finally, tuck the end beneath itself (as shown) and lay it alongside the two parts of the other rope. Tighten carefully so that all the knot parts bed down snugly together.

Heaving Line Bend

This quick and simple knot attaches a lightweight throwing line (or "messenger") to the bight or eye of a heavier hawser that is to be hauled into position. It was first mentioned in a seamanship manual of 1912.

1 Make a bight in the hawser that has to be hauled.

2 Take the lighter line and lay it over the bight.

3 Divert the working end to one side (the left in this instance), taking it around and beneath the standing part of the bight and then bringing it over its own standing part.

4 Take the working end beneath the short leg of the bight.

5 Bring the working end back to the lefthand side of the knot, tucking it finally beneath itself as shown. Note that the finished shot shows the reverse side of the completed knot.

Bowline Bend

In wet natural fibre ropes at sea, when even simple knots could be relied upon to hold, it was recommended that hawsers should be joined with a pair of interlocked bowlines, and that still holds good – literally – in some of today's cordage. The advantage of the bowline is that it does not slip or jam even under tension. This bend can be used for lines of dissimilar diameters, constructions and materials, but the two loops may be weakened where their interlinked elbows cross and rub against one another.

1 Make the initial overhand loop that will cinch the completed knot and tuck the working end up through it.

3 Tuck the working end down through the loop and pull the working end to tighten the knot.

2 Pass the working end around behind the standing part of the line.

4 Make an overhand loop with a second line and tuck the working end through the first bowline.

5 Pass the working end up through the second loop and under the standing part of the line.

6 Tuck this working end down through the second loop and pull the working end to tighten the knot.

Twin Bowline Bend

This alternative to the bowline bend avoids the sharp elbows of the latter knot and is stronger for that reason as it avoids the risk of chafing and rubbing.

1 Arrange the two lines parallel, with the working ends opposed.

2 Form the loop that is characteristic of bowlines in the standing part of one of the lines, as shown.

3 Tuck the other working end up through the loop and pass it around the back of the standing part.

4 Tuck the end down through the loop to complete the first bowline.

5 Turn the half-completed knot end-for-end and begin again with an identical loop.

6 Take the end and tuck it as before, up through the loop and around the standing part.

7 Tuck the end down through the loop to complete the second bowline, ensuring that the working ends are at least as long as those illustrated (and preferably longer). The standing parts will each take an equal part of the strain upon the loaded knot.

Pedigree Cow Hitch

This is a useful knot for a pull that is more or less at right angles to the point of attachment. Put it to work to start lashings or to suspend garden shed and garage impedimenta from the roof.

1 Take the working end around and down, from front to back of the anchorage point.

2 Bring the end around in front of its own standing part.

3 Take the end back up behind the foundation and bring it down in front once again.

4 Tuck the end through the bight, the result being a fairly useless common cow hitch.

5 Now tuck the working end back through the basic knot to secure and transform it.

Cow Hitch Variant

This is an even stronger and more secure version than the pedigree cow hitch. Although similar to the pedigree cow hitch, which was an innovation from the fresh mind of Harry Asher, the cow hitch variant was published in 1995 by Robert Pont of France, who first spotted it in Quebec and named it the Piwich knot after the child (Piwich Kust of the Bois Brule tribe) who tied it. Use it as a bag knot, or to suspend lockets, amulets and similar items of jewellery from a neck lanyard.

1 Take the working end once around the point of attachment.

2 Make a single half hitch with the working end around the line's standing part.

3 Take the working end across the front and pass it up (in this instance, to the left) behind the anchorage point.

4 Bring the working end down in front and tuck it down beside the standing part of the line, taking it through the enclosing turn.

Buntline Hitch

In effect, this is two half hitches with the second one inside the first, the working end being trapped against whatever it is tied around. This knot is for situations where the line flaps about with a tendency to shake less secure knots loose (for example, running rigging and flag halyards). A buntline was used to brail up square-sails, which flogged unmercifully, and so a very secure knot was needed. Tied in flat material, it turns out to be the common four-in-hand necktie knot that around 1860 superseded bowties for men.

1 Pass the working end through or around the anchorage point from front to back.

2 Take the end across the front and bring it around the back in a figure of eight layout.

3 Pass the end completely across the loop that has been formed.

4 Continue to take the end around to the back of the arrangement.

5 Tuck the working end through from back to front, as shown, thus forming two half hitches.

Clove Hitch, Tied in a Bight

The ease with which this knot can be tied makes it a popular one, but it comes adrift if pulled and jerked about. Then again, it can also jam, so consider adding a drawloop. Use it to suspend objects by means of lanyards or to secure a light boat to a bollard. Ashore, this knot was once known as a builder's knot.

1 Make an overhand loop at any convenient point in the line.

2 Add an underhand loop further along the line, so that the pair consists of two opposing halves.

3 Arrange the two loops so that they are the same size and close together.

4 Rotate the two loops a little in opposite directions, in order to overlap them.

5 Insert the rail, spar, rope or other foundation through both loops and pull either or both ends to tighten the resulting hitch.

Clove Hitch, Tied with a Working End

When this knot can be neither dropped over a bollard or stanchion nor slipped on to the end of a rail, or it is to be fastened to a ring, it must be tied this way.

1 Pass the working end around the anchorage point from front to back.

2 Bring the end forward and diagonally up across the front of the standing part (in this instance from right to left).

3 Take the working end down the back of the anchorage, so as to trap the standing part.

4 Then tuck the end up beneath the diagonal (forming what looks like a letter N, or its mirror-image).

5 Use a drawloop if an easy quick-release is required. Pull the standing part to tighten the knot.

Ground Line Hitch

This is a simple and easily tied knot to hitch a thin cord on to a thicker one. It is a tried and trusted hitch that has been used by cod fishermen on their trawl nets and as a picket line hitch by horse soldiers and wilderness pioneers. It can be used in the end of a coil of line to keep it all together, and is suitable for all kinds of cordage or other pliable materials. Add a drawloop for quick release, provided the knot is only intended to hold inanimate objects and the pull is a steady one.

1 Pass the working end around the foundation from front to back.

2 Bring the end forward again (in this instance, to the left of its own standing part).

3 Take the working end up and diagonally across the front of the work.

4 Pass the working end down behind the foundation to emerge at the front and to the right of the standing part.

5 Pull up the standing part to create an upper bight.

6 Tuck the working end through the newly created bight and then pull down on the standing part to trap it.

Gaff Topsail Halyard Bend

A legacy from the days of wooden ships, tarred ropes and large canvas sails, even the name of this knot evokes an image of blustering storms and sea spray. However, this is a misleading name since this knot is actually a hitch, an oddity that comes from the fact that sailors, by some unwritten rule, always talked of "bending" ropes to rings or spars. It is sufficiently secure under a steady pull at right angles to the point of attachment.

1 Take the working end of the rope or other line up behind the rail or spar and then bring it down in front.

2 Pass the end up behind the anchorage once again, completing a turn.

3 Bring the working end down in front once more, making a full round turn, and take it behind its own standing part.

4 Finally tuck the end up (in this instance from left to right) beneath both parts of the round turn.

Rolling Hitch

An elaboration of the clove hitch, this is intended to cope with a lengthwise pull. The two diagonal riding turns must go on the side of the object from which the pull will be applied.

1 Pass the working end around the anchorage from front to back.

2 Take the end up and diagonally across the front of the standing part.

3 Bring the working end down behind the work once more, bringing it out to emerge between the diagonal and the standing part.

4 Create a second diagonal turn, snugly beside the first one (and closest to the standing part), before passing the end down behind the work once more.

5 Tuck the working end up beneath the last diagonal turn only and lever it tight.

Knute Hitch

This simple, and no doubt ancient, knot was named by American master rigger Brion Toss in 1990. It attaches a lanyard or halyard to anything with a small eye, so safeguarding objects such as pocket knives or other tools, securing a sail or fastening a curtain tie-back.

2 Push the bight through any hole that is barely bigger than the doubled cord.

1 Make a small bight in the working end of the lanyard.

3 Tuck the end (with a stopper knot added to it) through the bight and pull on the standing part to tighten.

Pile Hitch

Little known – and often not considered a "proper" knot – this simple hitch is tied more quickly than it can be described. It is ideal for attaching barrier ropes to posts and rails where the bight or loop can be passed over the top, for crowd control or to isolate road works. John Smith, an active member of the The International Guild of Knot Tyers, suggests that, if there were to be only one knot in the world, it would have to be this one – for it can (as he demonstrates) also be ingeniously adapted into a knot, bend, binding or loop.

1 Make a bight at any selected point in the rope or line.

2 Pass the bight beneath both standing parts, and loop it over the post, stanchion or peg. Both legs of the line may then be led in different directions.

Double Pile Hitch

John Smith devised this double pile hitch as an alternative to the rolling hitch to enable a lengthways pull.

1 Make a bight at any selected point in the rope or cord.

2 Pass the bight around the post, stanchion, peg or other item used as an anchorage point.

3 Take the bight beneath the two standing parts to make a turn.

4 Lead the bight further around the anchorage to complete a round turn.

5 Bring the bight beneath both standing parts and pass it over the anchorage. This hitch is designed to cope with a load from one or both of the standing parts and towards the bight.

45

Turle Knot

For angled or offset eyed hooks and flies, this classic anglers' knot was published in 1841 and later popularized by Major Turle of Newton Stacey in Hampshire, England. Since a few people have now begun mistakenly to call it the turtle knot, this puts the record straight.

1 Pass the working end of the monofilament or braid through the eye of the hook or other object.

2 Lead the end around the shank of the hook and across the standing part to form a loop.

3 Tuck the end to create a short-lived half hitch.

4 Then finally tuck the working end to tie an overhand knot.

True Lover's Knot

One of the weaker angling knots (50 to 70 per cent), this hitch attaches monofilament or braided plastic-coated wire to a lure.

1 Tie an overhand knot and then pass the working end through the ring.

2 Tuck the end back through the knot alongside the standing part.

3 Adjust the ring loop to the required size; a small loop will allow the lure freedom to move realistically.

4 Tie a twin overhand knot with the working end, around the standing part of the line.

5 Arrange the second knot so that it lies snugly embedded against the first knot, then pull on the standing end to tighten the entire assembly.

KNOTS & COILS

The word "knot" has a specific meaning, apart from its general use for any cordage entanglement. Strictly speaking, it refers only to those that are not bends or hitches, namely stopper knots, shortenings, loops and bindings, as well as anything tied in string or other small material, such as cotton or thread. Stopper cordage knots may be used to prevent fraying but their function is primarily to prevent the cord pulling out of a pulley-block, fairlead or other opening. Shortenings are temporary devices, intended to avoid cutting rope that must later be reused. Bindings can be makeshift quick seizings or semi-permanent lashings, while slide-and-grip knots are remarkable shock-absorbing contrivances. The coils at the end of the chapter should be used for storing lengths of rope, hung on pegs well above the floor.

Ashley's Stopper Knot

The overhand knot, and figure-of-eight knot, despite their increasing bulks, will all pull through a hole of about the same diameter. For a fatter stopper, use this knot devised by Clifford Ashley sometime around 1910 after he had spied a lumpy knot, which he did not recognize, aboard a boat in the local oyster fishing fleet. This was the outcome, hence his name for it (the oysterman's stopper knot). Later, when he was able to see the mystery knot close up, it proved to be nothing but a wet and badly swollen figure-of-eight knot; but Ashley's new stopper knot has survived to become a minor classic.

1 Immobilizing the end, throw an overhand loop in the standing part of the line.

2 Take the standing part of the line beneath the loop.

3 Pull a bight through the loop to create an overhand knot with a drawloop.

4 Bring the working end up and through from the back of the bight (no other way will do). Pull the standing part down until the bight traps the end tightly against the knot.

Figure-of-Eight Knot

Favoured by dinghy sailors for the ends of jib leads and main sheets, this quick and simple knot has a bit more bulk than an overhand knot and is more easily untied – but it will escape through holes of roughly the same size. In its untightened form, this familiar knot has long been associated with faithful love – an emblem of interwoven affection.

1 Make a small bight at the end of the line and impart half a twist to turn it into a loop.

2 Impart an extra half twist to bring about the figure-of-eight shape that gives this knot its name.

3 Begin to pull the working end through the loop from the top. If you wish to leave a drawloop, stop at this stage.

4 Draw the working end right the way through to complete a common figure-of-eight knot. To tighten this knot, tug first on both ends to remove slack from the knot; then pull on just the standing part, pulling the end over and trapping it against the top of the knot.

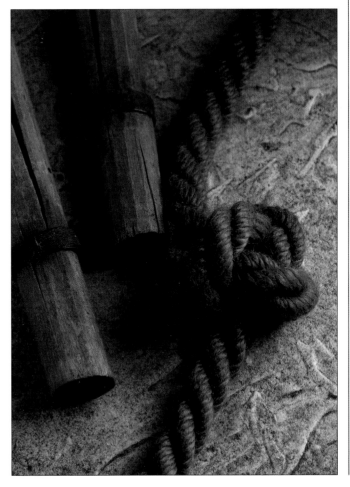

Munter Friction Hitch

An effective means of abseiling (rappelling), belaying or absorbing the energy of a fall, this friction hitch for kernmantel rope also reverses to yield slack or apply tension when needed. The rope is pressed around and through the karibiner and will break the fall of a climber by locking up, in much the same way that a car seat belt locks. Although it can be used for abseiling (rappelling), this is not generally recommended as the practice can be hard on the rope, eventually causing it to "burn". The munter friction hitch was introduced in 1974, and is also known as the Italian hitch and sliding ring hitch.

1 Use the climbing rope with an appropriate size and quality of karabiner.

2 Make a loop (exactly as illustrated) in the climbing rope.

3 Unscrew (if necessary) and open the gate of the karabiner.

4 Hook upwards with the karabiner to incorporate the climbing rope.

5 Then pass the karabiner through the initial loop from back to front (no other way will work).

6 When completed, this hitch is revealed as a dynamic crossing knot. The finished shot shows this knot from the rear side.

Double Munter Friction Hitch

Canadian rock and building climber Robert Chisnall devised and publicized this variation of the munter friction hitch. The additional turn around the karabiner creates greater friction and consequently more control over the load line. This is ideal for smaller diameter rope, which often needs more friction.

1 Choose an appropriate size and quality of karabiner to use with the climbing rope.

2 Make a double loop in the climbing rope, exactly as illustrated.

3 Hook upwards with the karabiner to incorporate the climbing rope.

4 Then pass the karabiner through the initial double loop from back to front as shown (no other way will work).

5 When completed, this hitch exerts more friction, and so will support greater loads than the basic knot.

Sheepshank

The sheepshank temporarily shortens a length of rope. It will bridge an obviously damaged or a suspect section of rope, taking the strain upon the other two standing parts.

1 Fold the rope and fold it again, shortening it as required, into a flattened "S" or "Z" shape with two bights.

2 Make an incomplete overhand knot – known as a marlinespike hitch – in one standing part.

3 Pull the adjacent bight through the marlinespike hitch in a locking tuck that goes over-under-over the rope.

4 Turn the half-finished knot end-for-end and make another marlinespike hitch in the other standing part.

5 Insert the remaining bight over-under-over, securing the nearby hitch, and gently tighten both ends of the knot until they are snug and firm. Ensure that the load falls equally on all three standing parts (unless one is damaged, in which case it must lie between the other two and be slightly slacker than them).

Square Knot

Dressing gown (bath robe) cords or other waist-ties may be fastened with this knot, allowing the ends to hang down stylishly. It is best, however, in a knotted scarf, when the four-panelled knot neatly fills the V-shaped space in an open blouse or shirt. Because there is already a square knot in the United States (which the British call the reef knot), Americans refer to this knot by several other names, including the rustler's knot, the Japanese crown knot, the Japanese success knot, the Chinese cross knot, and the Chinese good luck knot.

1 Make a bight in one of two cords, or one end of a single cord, and pass it around the other cord or end.

2 Lead the second cord up behind the initial bight in the other cord.

3 Bring the second cord down in front of the first one.

4 Pass the first working end over the front of the second to make a locking tuck through the open bight. Flatten and tighten this knot by pulling a bit at a time on each of the four strands that emerge from the knot.

Good Luck Knot

For a robust knot, easy to tie and tighten, this has a striking finished appearance. Use it for gift-wrapped parcels or simply hang it from a belt as a novel chatelaine for keys (keychain). The appearance of this knot will be enhanced if, between the three large loops, the four small ones are left open.

1 Middle a single length of cord and make a narrow bight in it.

2 Pull out and retain a second bight in the lefthand leg of the cord.

3 Pull out a matching bight in the righthand leg of the cord.

4 Lay both standing parts of the cord up and over the lefthand bight.

5 Take the lefthand bight and lay it over the upper bight.

6 Take the upper bight and lay it down over the righthand bight.

7 Tuck the righthand bight over and through beneath the two standing parts of the cord.

8 Without distorting it in any way, carefully tighten the resulting four-part crown knot.

9 Bring the lefthand bight down and cross the lower bight up over it.

10 Lay the righthand bight up and over the lower bight.

11 Lead the two standing parts of the cord down in a final locking tuck through the vacant bight. Tighten the second crown knot atop the first one.

Wrapped & Reef Knotted Coil

Rope coiled this way and secured with reef (square) knots has a good chance of surviving any journey tangle-free. This is a quick and simple arrangement that serves to prevent all sorts of frustrating entanglements. It works for thick rope and smaller cordage, and is easy to untie when the rope is required.

1 Bring the two ends of the coiled rope close together, and tie a half-knot (with longer ends than are illustrated).

2 Then add a second half-knot (of opposite handedness) to complete a reef (square) knot.

3 Wrap both ends away from the reef (square) knot, with identical helixes, so as to secure the coil.

4 Where the two ends meet opposite the original reef (square) knot, tie another half-knot.

5 Then add a second half-knot (of opposite handedness) to complete a second reef (square) knot.

Alpine Coil

This is the method of securing a coil of rope for transport that is traditionally preferred by climbers and cavers.

1 Bring the two ends of the coiled rope close together.

2 Bend one end back to create a bight about 15–20 cm/6–8 in long.

3 Wrap the other end around the coiled rope, including the bight.

4 Ensure that the second wrapping turn traps and holds the initial turn.

5 Wrap fairly tightly and keep each succeeding turn snug.

6 Complete at least six wrapping turns, then tuck the working end through the bight (pulling upon the other end to secure it).

Figure-of-Eight Coil

This is the storekeeper's way of hanging coils up out of harm's way. Coiling the rope double is the trick that makes this coil fast and effective, with a practical loop to hang it by. Ropes travelling in the back of a car can always be coiled this way as they can be held in place by securing the loop around a fixed object. It is, like many of the coils, quick and easy to untie, if required in an emergency.

1 Middle the rope prior to coiling and then coil it doubled.

2 Bring the bight back upon itself so as to create a loop.

3 Lead the working bight around the back of the coil to the other side.

4 Finally tuck it up through its own loop (and the entire coil), from front to back, to make a loop from which to hang it.

Fireman's Coil

This method of forming a coil with a useful hanging loop is probably the most basic coil and deserves to be better known.

1 Bring the two ends of the coiled rope close together.

2 With one of the ends, make an overhand small loop.

3 Pass the working end through the coil and behind it, and make a bight.

4 Tuck the bight up through the loop, from behind, and gently pull it tight. Suspend the coil from this loop.

BINDINGS & LOOPS

There are two kinds of binding knot. The first is around an object with a wide diameter, where a cord, strap or fabric is wound one or more times and the two ends are then securely tied together (for example, packing parcels, securing a cloth covering to a homemade jar of preserves or applying a first aid tourniquet). The second is for narrow diameters, when a special constricting knot is applied to grip and hold with its own internal friction (for example, to prevent the cut end of a rope from fraying or to attach a hose to a tap).

A loop knot may be used like a hitch, but placed over a post or rail (rather than tied around it), the advantage being that it is easily removed again for re-use. Running knots or nooses, useful for parcels, may have originated as snares to catch animals and birds for food. Some loops are tied in the bight, others in the end of cordage.

Sack/Miller's Knot

This was used in the days when grain and other granular or powdered materials were bagged up in sacks. It cannot be tied in the bight but a drawloop may be left to prevent possible damage to the bag if the knot is cut.

1 Drape a short length of cord around the neck of the bag or sack with the short end hanging down in front of the bag.

2 Move the short end at the front over to the left.

3 Wrap the longer working end up and over the neck of the bag or sack, from front to back, taking care to trap the short end in place.

4 Take the working end down around the back of the bag and bring it up at the front again.

5 Tuck the end down through the space retained between the first and second wrapping turns and pull it snug and tight. Leave a drawloop, if preferred.

Reef Knot (Square Knot)

This flat and symmetrical knot of two interlocked bights was known to the ancient Egyptians, Greeks and Romans. With twin drawloops, it becomes the double reef (square) bow, a more secure way to tie shoe-laces. It is strictly a binding knot, reliable only when pressed against something else and tied in both ends of the same material, so restrict its use to bandages and all sorts of parcels (including reefing the sails of small craft).

NOTE – Never use it as a bend.

1 Bring two ends of the same cord together, in this case left over right.

2 Tie a half-knot and see how the two entwined knot parts spiral to the left, anticlockwise (counterclockwise).

3 Bring the two ends back together, but this time right over left.

4 Tie a second half-knot. Note that the two entwined parts helix to the right, anticlockwise (counterclockwise), the opposite of the first half-knot.

Constrictor Knot, Tied with an End

The constrictor knot can be the best of binding knots. Use it with or without a drawloop as a semi-permanent seizing on rope's ends, hose-pipes, and for every odd job imaginable. The ancient Greeks may have used it for surgical slings, and it could well be the "gunner's knot" that in later centuries seized the necks of flannel-bag gunpowder cartridges for muzzle-loading artillery. It was re-discovered and popularized by Clifford Ashley in 1944. Use this tying method when the end of the foundation rope, spar or whatever, is not easily accessible. If you wish to remove a constrictor – without nicking or scarring whatever lies beneath it – you must carefully sever the overriding diagonal with a sharp knife, and then the knot will drop neatly off in two curly cut segments.

1 Take a short length of cord or twine (hard-laid to bind softer objects, such as rope; soft and stretchy for unyielding foundations) and arrange it around whatever is to be tied.

2 Bring the working end of the binding cord up and across to the right over its own standing part.

3 Lead the end down at the back and up once more at the front.

4 Tuck the working end beneath the diagonal made earlier, completing a clove hitch.

5 Locate and loosen the upper lefthand knot part, preparatory to tucking in the working end.

6 Bring the working end across and tuck it from left to right through the loosened bight. Pull both ends in opposite directions to tighten this knot as hard as possible, when the ends may be cut off quite close to the knot.

Constrictor Knot, Tied in the Bight

This is another example of the excellent constrictor knot. Tie it more quickly this way when the end of the foundation rope, spar, or whatever, is accessible. When pulled tight it will lock securely. With practice, a constrictor knot tied by this method can be applied quicker than the eye can follow the actions.

1 Lead the working end of a short length of cord or twine, from front to back, over the object to be seized.

2 Lift the working end so as to complete a full turn.

3 Pull a fairly long bight down from the lower part of the turn just made.

4 Lift the bight and half-twist it (as shown) to place it over the end of the foundation.

5 Heave on both ends, as strongly as the cord or twine will withstand, to tighten the knot; then cut off the ends close to the knot.

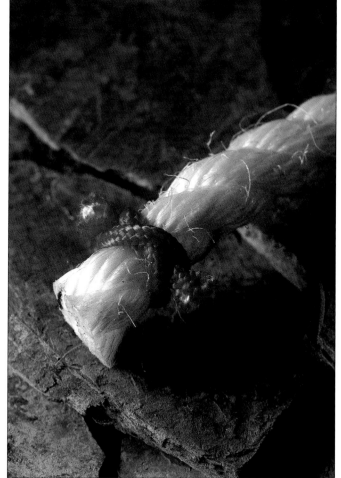

Double Constrictor Knot

This variation of the constrictor knot has extra internal friction and grip; it is also more suitable for binding objects with a larger diameter, or when the objects are an awkward shape and will not automatically pull together. When tying a particularly awkward package and hands are not enough to tighten this seizing as much as required, attach each end of the cord to a screwdriver or similar handle by means of a pile hitch to apply extra leverage.

1 Wrap the cord around the item to be secured. Bring the working end diagonally up and take it across over its own standing part.

2 Lead the working end down behind the work and then up in front once more, taking care to keep between the standing part and the initial turn.

3 Take the working end up and around the foundation again, doubling the characteristic diagonal that overlays the single version of this knot.

4 Put the working end directly down behind, to emerge at the front (on the righthand side of its standing part).

5 Tuck the end through the two turns so it is parallel and to the right of its own standing part.

6 Locate and loosen the upper lefthand part of this almost completed knot, preparatory to the final tuck.

7 Bring the working end across and tuck it from left to right through the loosened bight.

8 Pull the knot as tight as possible and cut the ends off close to the knot.

Bowline

Once this knot was used for attaching a line from the bow of a ship to the weather leech of a square-sail, holding it closer to the wind, and thus preventing it being taken aback (blown inside out). Nowadays the same bowline (pronounced "boh-linn") is used, misused and abused for innumerable other jobs from tying parcels to tree surgery. Among its advantages are that it does not slip, loosen or jam. It remains a time-honoured knot, which may, however, need to have its working end tied or taped to the adjacent loop leg for added security.

1 Bring the working end across the standing part of the rope to form an overhand loop.

2 Rotate the hand clockwise and so produce a smaller loop in the standing part of the rope.

3 Ensure that the working end points upwards (from back to front) through the small loop.

4 Lead the end around behind the standing part of the rope.

5 Then tuck it back down through the small loop, this time from front to back.

6 Arrange the completed knot with a long end (longer than shown) and consider further securing it with tape, a half hitch or other extra fastening.

Eskimo Bowline

This variation on the orthodox bowline is sometimes referred to as the Boas bowline. The Arctic explorer Sir John Ross (1777–1856) brought an Inuit (Eskimo) sled back to England that had been presented to him by Inuits. It contained numerous such knots in its rawhide lashings, evidence that this was a genuine Inuit knot. The sled is now in the basement of the Museum of Mankind, London. As it is more secure than the common bowline, especially in synthetic lines, it is worth learning.

1 Make an underhand loop in one end of the rope.

2 Bring the standing end down behind the loop, creating an incomplete overhand knot.

3 Lift the standing part of the rope up slightly within the loop.

4 Then make a locking tuck (over/under/over) with the working end of the rope.

5 Let the working end be pulled into a bight by the marlinespike hitch.

6 Draw the marlinespike hitch down over the bight. Note the untypical face of this bowline, when tightened, with its distinctive trefoil crown.

Spanish Bowline

The splayed loops of this ancient knot can hoist a person aloft, or lower them safely, with a leg thrust through each. It is used by fire brigades, coastguards and rescue teams and is also known as the chair knot. However, anyone being lifted would have to hold firmly to the standing parts of the rope at chest level so as not to be tipped out, so exercise extreme caution when using this and other improvised rescue knots. This bowline is a tried and trusted old knot with a maritime background.

1 Middle – or make a long bight in – the rope, doubling it to create two twin loops.

2 Impart an upward, anticlockwise (counterclockwise) half twist to the lefthand loop.

3 Impart a matching upward (but clockwise) mirror-image half twist to the righthand loop.

4 Keeping the previously created twists, pass the lefthand loop through the righthand loop.

5 Rearrange, or allow the rope to open out, to the simple layout shown.

6 Enlarge the lower crossing turn, producing two bights.

7 Lift and half twist both lower loops. Pass them through the upper loops.

8 Pull the two loops outwards until they are the required size; pull down on the standing parts to tighten the knot. If one end is close to the knot, secure it to the adjacent standing part with a double overhand knot.

Figure-of-Eight Loop

Referred to by sailormen once upon a time as a Flemish loop, the figure-of-eight loop was viewed by them with disfavour because it tended to jam in wet hemp or manilla ropes and could not easily be untied after loading. Cavers and climbers now prefer this versatile alternative to the bowline. It is easily tied – even by an uncertain beginner – and readily checked by a team leader (in the poorest light and the worst weather). Tie the working end to the standing part for added security.

1 Make a generous bight in the end of the cord or rope.

2 Impart half a twist in the bight to create twin loops, as shown.

3 Add an extra half-twist to the loops already produced, as shown.

4 Tuck the bight through the twin loops and work the completed knot neatly snug and tight.

Manharness Knot

This is an ancient knot, although as recently as 1992 American Mike Storch recommended a series of these knots spaced out along a picket line to tether horses. It is tied in the bight.

1 Make an anticlockwise (counterclockwise) overhand loop.

2 Bring the upper section of line around to the back of the loop.

3 Press the righthand side of the original loop to the left beneath the middle (rearward) knot part.

4 Then pull it further left, over the lefthand side of the loop.

5 Hold onto the loop and pull the knot to tighten it.

Alpine Butterfly

This is a European mountaineering classic middleman's tie-on. If, as A.P. Herbert (1890–1971) wrote in a poem, "the bowline is the king of knots", then the Alpine butterfly, added Scouting's ropework writer John Sweet, must surely be the queen. Its other name, given to it by Clifford Ashley, is the lineman's loop. It is tied in the bight.

1 Lay a bight of rope over one hand at the point where the knot is required.

2 Lead the working part of the rope around the hand a second time to complete one round turn.

3 Add a third turn with the rope around the hand.

4 Pick up the righthand turn and relocate it between the other two turns.

5 Pick up the new righthand turn and leap-frog it across to become the lefthand turn.

6 Tuck the lefthand rope part through (from left to right) beneath the other two turns.

7 Pull out a bight of the required size and then pull on both standing parts of the rope to tighten the knot.

Bowstring Knot

Limited adjustment makes this knot suitable for small roles such as tightening or slackening tent guy lines or washing lines. It has been used to improvise the sliding loop on American cowboys' lassoes and the lariats of the Spanish vaqueros; while the ancient Briton, Lindow Man – whose 2,000-year-old mummified remains are now displayed in the British Museum, London – was strangled with a similar knot.

1 With the working end of a rope, make a clockwise underhand loop.

2 Tuck the working end through the loop to produce an overhand knot.

3 Take the working end through the end compartment of the overhand knot, ensuring that the over-under sequence is precisely as shown (no other way will do).

4 Tighten the knot, adding a small stopper knot to prevent the end from pulling free.

Midshipman's Hitch

This is a slide-and-grip knot, which may be grasped and slid by hand to where it is required (after which it holds firm), making it suitable for tensioning guy lines, stays or shrouds. The name implies a Royal Navy origin.

1 Make a clockwise overhand loop of approximately the required size.

2 Bring the working end around and tuck it from the back through the loop just formed.

3 Take the working end up and begin a wrapping turn, which must cross and trap its own earlier turn.

4 Bring the working end once again through the loop and continue to wrap it (towards the standing part).

5 Take the working end up and around the standing part, so that two turns now diagonally overlay and trap the original turn.

6 Lead the working end outside the loop and take it from left to right across the front of the standing part.

7 Finally, create a half hitch around the standing part of the line and tighten it so that it lies alongside the other riding turns.

Arbor Knot

Primarily a knot attaching
monofilament or braid to an
arbor (a reel or spool), this knot
is also used as a shock-absorbing
slide-and-grip knot when securing
a line to a hook or lure.

1 Make a bight near to one end of the
monofilament, braid or other line.

2 Keeping the two parallel line parts
close together, form a small loop by
laying the working end across them.

3 Continue by taking the working end
down behind the emerging knot.

4 Bring the end up out of the loop and
complete a round turn of the two
bight parts.

5 Take the working end down behind
the knot once more.

6 Complete a second turn, keeping the
wrappings tight as they are tied.

7 Take a third turn with the working
end, ensuring that all are snug
against one another. Tighten the small
loop, and trap the end by pulling on one
of the large loop legs.

Adjustable Loop

Another creation from Canadian climber Robert Chisnall, this loop can easily be shifted by hand in either direction – but it seizes when loaded. A safety feature of this knot (and of all slide-and-grip knots) is that shock loading will cause it to slide until friction reduces the load to a manageable percentage, when it will hold.

1 Make a loop with the working end laid over the standing part.

2 With the working end, take a turn around the standing part.

3 Take a second turn around the standing part with the working end.

4 Now pass the working end around both legs of the loop.

5 Finally, tuck the working end beneath the second wrapping turn.

Portuguese Bowline

Old-time sailormen were a polyglot tribe who shipped aboard any vessel that would have them, so knot names spread haphazardly. Felix Reisenberg called this a French bowline; whereas Clifford Ashley, who spotted it aboard Portuguese boats in his home town of New Bedford, Massachusetts, gave it the current name. It was used as a kind of boatswain's chair, with the crewman's legs through one loop and his back supported by the other one.

1 Form a small overhand loop with the working end of the rope.

2 Make a large loop in the same direction and of roughly the required working size.

3 As the working end approaches the smaller loop, take it behind.

4 Bring it up and through the cinch as if tying a common bowline.

5 Take the end around the back of the standing part of the rope.

6 Finally, tuck the end down through the cinch and tighten the resulting knot around the two trapped loop parts. Ensure the end is longer than illustrated.

Portuguese Bowline with Splayed Loops

A couple of these versatile knots will sling a plank or ladder as an improvised work platform, but note that each one of the two loops can pull slack from the other. Do not use this knot in circumstances where this may prove an undesirable feature. An illustration of this knot appeared in *Tratado de Apparelho do Navio*, (1896), Lisbon, and Clifford Ashley reports having first seen it used aboard Portuguese ships.

1 Arrange the line as shown in the illustration above.

2 Reduce the size of the lower loop, secure the lefthand bight, and bring the working end around to create a second loop on the righthand side of the emerging knot.

3 Tuck the working end up through the small central loop and then take the end around behind the standing part of the rope.

4 Finally, tuck the end down through the central loop or cinch. Adjust the two working loops to the required size, and then begin to tighten the familiar bowline layout.

81

MATS, PLAITS, RINGS, SLINGS & THINGS

Knots are like tools. It is possible to muddle along with four or five, using and misusing them for every task imaginable. The best strategy, however, is to acquire a full and varied repertoire of bends, hitches and other contrivances, so that you always have precisely the correct combination for the job in hand. There are many knots, bends and hitches that are used only infrequently; but, when they are called for, nothing else will do the job as efficiently. What follows is a selection of these occasional knots.

Barrel Sling

Use this split form of the overhand knot to hoist or lower an open barrel, cask or drum that is partly full. The working end must be secured to the standing part of the rope, and care must also be taken to ensure that the bottom loop is unable to slip from beneath the load. This sling appears barely adequate for the job, yet it was once a handy favourite with crews shifting cargoes of tubs, casks and barrels.

1 Place the lifting line beneath the load and tie a half knot on top.

2 Split the half knot in two and work each knot part down over the load.

3 Pull both legs of the divided knot snug around the load.

4 Finally, tie a bowline in the shorter end to the standing part.

Plank Sling

A grown-up relative of pole lashings but made with ropes rather than cords. A couple of plank slings will improvise a working platform.

1 Place one end of the rope beneath the plank or other staging.

2 Push an extra bight beneath the plank, making an "S" or "Z" shape.

3 Bring one end of the rope across and tuck it through the bight on the opposite side of the plank.

4 Take the other end across and tuck it through the opposite bight.

5 Adjust and tighten the sling so that the tips of the bights are just above the edges of the plank, on the working surface; then tie the shorter end to the standing part of the rope.

Marline Hitching

Marline hitching looks identical to half hitching, but it is in fact very different. Try sliding both kinds off: half hitching collapses to nothing, which means that it can be tied in the bight, while marline hitching emerges as a string of overhand knots (and so requires a working end). This method tends to cling better during the tying process, but is somewhat slower to do than the simpler half hitching. Use it to lash up a garden hammock for winter storage or a carpet when moving house, and to parcel any other awkwardly long load.

1 Start with a sliding noose around the goods, tied from a small fixed loop with the working end passed through it.

2 Tie an overhand knot around the parcel, using the working end.

3 Pull the overhand knot tight, when, unlike mere half hitching, the extra friction will tend to hold the surrounding knot in place.

4 Add a series of such overhand knots, spaced evenly along the length of the parcel. Turn the work over and return to the starting place with a series of crossing knots and tie off.

Underhand Loop Hitching

The spine that emerges from this covering is a kind of chain stitch best fitted for a thicker ring. This – and other ring hitchings – may be executed in fairly fine twines and cords by needleworkers or by rope workers in wool, cottons or silks. They are also applied with substantial leather thongs by leather workers. It is a very versatile technique. This kind of hitching looks similar to a knitting stitch, but knitted items can unravel, whereas this pattern is composed of individual knots, each of which is separately and securely tied and, unlike knitting stitches, is not reliant on the preceding knots or stitches. Use it on light pulls or curtain cords.

1 Take a turn around the ring with the cord and cross the two parts, the standing end up and the working end down.

2 Form a clockwise underhand loop with the working part of the cord.

3 Pass the working end through the ring (from right to left).

4 Tuck the end up through the underhand loop, and draw the knotting snug and tight.

5 Continue to wrap around the ring and tuck through underhand loops.

6 Reproduce the looped and tucked pattern until the ring is covered.

Simple Chain

This simple chain will shorten an over-long rope or cord by about one-third. It will also embellish a fine twine, to make an attractive cord to retain reading glasses, for example.

1 Cast an anticlockwise (counter-clockwise) overhand loop with a long working end.

2 Lay the working end beneath the loop and pull a bight (from back to front) through it; then pull the resulting knot tight.

3 Pull a second bight in the working end through the first bight and pull it tight.

4 Similarly, pull a third bight through the second bight and pull it tight.

5 Continue pulling, bight through bight, tightening each stage before going on to the next.

6 To finish the chain, simply tuck the working end through the preceding bight. This will secure the completed chain sufficiently.

Endless Simple Chain

This is a very neat way to join the ends of a simple chain, ensuring that it keeps the same shape even on the join. It makes an original bracelet, necklace or anklet, and it may even be used to frame a picture or mirror. The steps are illustrated in two different colours but this chain is usually made with two ends of one cord.

1 Bring the beginning and end of one or two simple chains together.

2 Tuck the final end – in this instance, the lefthand one – up through the starting loop (from the back to the front), alongside the standing end.

3 Take the working end up (from the back to the front) through its own loop, beside itself.

4 Pass the end to the right, down (from front to back) through the adjacent loop made by step 3.

5 Withdraw the standing end from the first of its tucks and replace it with the working end.

Three-Strand Braid

This is the most common type of braid. Lashings and lanyards can quickly be made from smaller stuff by this means; horses' tails or long human hair can also be made orderly with it.

1 Bind three strands together and separate them into a lefthand single strand and a righthand pair of strands.

2 Bring the outermost one of the righthand pair across (over the front) to lie inside and below the lefthand strand.

3 Take the outermost one of the lefthand pair of strands and bring it across (over the front) to lie inside and below the righthand strand.

4 Repeat step 2, pulling and tightening the work as it develops.

5 Repeat step 3, pulling with an even tension as the work develops.

6 Repeat step 2, always taking (as the latest working strand) the one of the pair furthest away.

7 Continue plaiting (braiding) with alternate strands until the desired length is reached. Knot or bind the ends securely together to prevent them from coming undone.

Four-Strand Braid

This makes a flat lashing or lanyard which, in stiff stuff, will result in a detailed network of ornamental openwork.

1 Middle two lengths of rope or cord, looping one over the other (as shown), and separating the four strands into a lefthand and a righthand pair.

2 Simultaneously, cross the lefthand pair of strands (left over right) and the righthand pair (also left over right).

3 Then cross the innermost two strands (right over left).

4 Repeat steps 2 and 3, with tension and tightness to ensure a symmetrical pattern develops.

5 Continue this process until the desired length has been reached. Bind the ends together.

Four-Strand Plait

Use good quality cords to make a lead for a small dog, a lavatory or light pull, or a waist-tie for an informal garment. This is the plait (braid) that may be seen attached to the handset of vintage telephones. It may also be used to quadruple the strength of smaller cordage when no thicker cord or rope is available.

1 Bind four strands together and sub-divide them into a lefthand and a righthand pair; then take the outer one of the righthand pair across (behind), tucking it up through and between the two lefthand strands, and returning it to lie inside and below its original righthand companion.

2 Similarly, lead the outer lefthand strand around behind, to emerge between the two righthand strands, and return to lie inside and below its lefthand partner.

3 Repeat step 1, continuing to pull and tighten the paired strands as the work progresses.

4 Repeat step 2, ensuring an even tension as the work develops.

5 Continue this regular plaiting (braiding) process, with alternate outer strands, until the required length is reached. Bind the ends together.

Three-Way Sheet Bend

For a three-way bridle of converging lines, consider this simple yet effective solution. It was first reported in 1990 by the Swedish marine artist and knotting writer Frank Rosenow, who spotted it while cruising in Greek waters.

1 Bring together three pieces of rope, which may be of dissimilar size and texture.

2 Make a bight in one of the lines – the larger or stiffer, if there is one.

3 Tuck both of the other lines up through the bight.

4 Wrap the two lines around the bight and tuck them beneath themselves, so that all three working ends are on the same side of the finished knot.

Round Mat

This knotted roundel can replace an ordinary mat, or it may be glued as ornamentation or embellishment to items as diverse as a collage picture or a drum majorette's uniform.

1 Middle a length of cord and cast an anticlockwise (counterclockwise) overhand loop in the working end.

2 Bring the working end down behind the loop and arrange a symmetrical pretzel layout.

3 Pick up the other end of the cord and tuck it diagonally (up and to the left) over/under/over.

4 Lead the working end around clockwise and tuck diagonally (down and to the right) under/over/under/over.

5 Tuck the end alongside the standing part. Follow the original lead around to double or triple the knot ply. Glue or stitch the end in place on the underside.

Carrick Mat

This can be used as an actual mat, or as a component of other art and craft work. Made around the hand, the same knot can form a necktie ring.

1 Cast a clockwise overhand loop in a length of cord or rope.

2 Bring the working end down over the original loop and arrange a pretzel layout.

3 Pass the working end around (from right to left), keeping it behind the standing part.

4 Tuck it clockwise around and through the knot going over/under/over/under.

5 Tuck the working end alongside and parallel to the standing part. Follow the original lead around to double or triple the knot ply.

Index